The First Great Myth of Legal Management is that It Exists

Tough Issues for Law Firm Managing Partners and Administrators

by

H. Edward Wesemann

First published by Author House 04/07/04

ISBN: 1-4184-1559-6 (e-book)
ISBN: 1-4184-1561-8 (Paperback)
ISBN: 1-4184-1560-X (Dust Jacket)

This book is printed on acid free paper.

Table of Contents

"Eighty percent of success is showing up."

Woody Allen

Introduction

"You must be present to win." You don't hear those words much any more. Before state lotteries and computer generated numbers, when most people's legal gambling was confined to charity drawings, it was common for the drawings to require that participants "must be present to win." That was okay with my father. He used to say that anyone who didn't show up for the drawing didn't deserve to win.

Woody Allen sort of said the same thing in his signature line, "Eighty percent of success is showing up." The point is that while consultants and academics try to make a big deal out of "how" law firms are managed, the fact is that most law firms simply aren't managed.

The lack of management is not particularly the fault of law firm managers. Actually, I'm not sure who to blame for the lack of management in most firms. We know that lawyers are highly individualistic and, as a species, tend not to play well with others. Perhaps it is because virtually all law firms are governed by committees and the only other organizations run by committees are those bastions of effective management – universities and governments. It could also be that lawyers, for all their supposed aggressiveness are, by and large, introverts and adverse to confrontation. So, to avoid confrontation, most law firms that, with great pride, proclaim themselves to be democratic are really consensus based.

Consensus means that the members of an organization talk about issues until they come up with a decision that everyone can accept. Consensus really means that every member effectively has a veto. If you're a partner in a law firm and you are opposed to an issue, just hold out and you can stall off a decision forever. I think lawyers get their love for consensus from the jury system where there has to be a unanimous verdict. It works with juries because the judge can lock them in a room and not let them go home or pursue their livelihood until they come to a decision. Take that away and watch the number of hung juries soar. The point is that the way law firms are organized and govern themselves makes it tough to come up with any decision, much less one that isn't a watered down lowest common denominator approach to problems and issues.

How is it then that law firms ever get anything done? How do they decide to open new offices or create new practice areas or merge with other law firms? The truth is, in just about every law firm I can think of, major actions are the result of one partner with a mission. In the firms that seem to be extraordinarily successful, that partner has a formal role in management and we call his mission vision and leadership.

This book is made up of 13 assorted small missions. Each came from an email that I sent to clients and friends during 2003. They are really random thought, not terribly strategic and certainly not coordinated. But for all their frustrations, managing law firms is about winning small battles and finding areas where members of legal management can take simple actions.

As a result, the law firm managers that are able to get their firms to do something – anything – usually wins. Like Woody said, eighty percent of success is showing up. Like my dad said, if you don't show up, you don't deserve to win.

"Success is the ability to go from one failure to another with no loss of enthusiasm."

Sir Winston Churchill

Firing Unprofitable Clients

As law firms attempt to drive greater profitability, it is common for partners to talk about "firing unprofitable clients." But few firms have the ability to distinguish the comparative profitability of clients and even fewer have the discipline to take action. The truth is that a law firm's client base goes a long way in determining its profit level, and improvement does not require a wholesale change of clients.

Defining Profitability

Most firms don't have the wherewithal to determine the profitability of their clients. Usually it is not because the firms lack the appropriate computer software or do not have access to the necessary data. Rather, the firms have a problem coming up with a common definition of what constitutes profitability. The difficulty is that law firms are made up of partners who are skilled advocates prepared to vigorously defend their clients regardless of their value to the firm.

Experience with countless firms trying to increase client profitability provides two simple lessons. First, there is no measure of client profitability with sufficient credibility to withstand attack by a skilled advocate. Lawyers earn their living using small flaws to defeat otherwise sound arguments. Spending a lot of time on a computer profitability model is not worth the effort. Secondly, when firms are looking for unprofitable clients, what they usually find is "the smaller the client, the smaller the profit."

Small Clients

By almost any standard, small clients – either individuals or businesses – are problematic for law firms. Being sensitive to the limited financial resources of small clients, rarely is all of the time required to perform work recorded by the working attorneys and while billing, small clients often are the most frequently written down.

After billing, small clients represent the greatest risk of bad debt write-off of all accounts receivable. Indeed when you review the accounts receivable delinquency lists of law firms, individuals and small or startup companies tend to be the largest offenders. And if a firm becomes aggressive in attempting to secure payment, small clients represent the greatest risk of a malpractice suit. In fact, the nuisance claims that law firms routinely buy-off are invariably brought by small clients. By the same token, small clients, by their sheer number present the greatest conflicts of interest.

Any firm that has attempted to trace where its entertainment expenses are going, particularly tickets to sporting events and usage of stadium lounges, will quickly note that small clients are entertained with a frequency disproportionate to their revenue contribution.

Finally, small clients do little to enhance the reputation of the firm and build the skill levels of its lawyers.

80/20 Rule

Rarely do law firms focus on the magnitude of small client issues. There is clearly a difference between clients that are small businesses but pay a large amount of money in fees and large businesses that do not pay much in fees. But the converse is more typically true, and, for all intents and purposes, small total fee amounts tend to be paid by small clients. In virtually every law firm 80% of the firm's revenues come from 20% or fewer of its clients. Or, conversely, if a law firm fired 80% of its clients it would only lose 20% of its revenue or less. Consider the impact on overhead expenses of eliminating 80% of the client base and focusing the firm's attention and service resources on the top 20% of its clients.

At this point, some partner in a law firm will point out that all large clients started out as small clients. Indeed, it seems that every law firm has one story of a large client that grew from being a small client. Usually the story involves a business starting in a garage. But rarely does a firm have more than one such story. Therefore, if a law firm can point to one such occasion…forget it…it will probably never happen again. Besides, when the client develops in size, it will be the target of competitors who will point out that the client has outgrown a law firm that serves small clients.

Taking Action

While it is easy to make an intellectual argument in favor of firing small clients, few firms are able to even begin culling their client list. In most firms, specific clients are the exclusive property of individual lawyers whose compensation is based on gross revenues, regardless of the cost of creating those revenues. It is hard to find someone to deliver the difficult message to a client the firm would rather not serve.

There are, however, some actions a firm can take which do not require the actual firing of a client:

- **Eliminate discounts**. Most businesses provide price discounts based on volume. But in law firms, often the lowest rates are charged to the smallest clients. With the next bill simply charge the client at full rates. Explain that the firm has large clients who expect to enjoy *most favored nation* rates, which forces the firm to bring the small client's rate up to standard. Either the client will pay the higher rates or they will seek other counsel—both good results.

5

- **Push work down.** Hand off small client relationships to a junior associate. The associate will charge lower rates and gain experience in client relations and billing management. A year later if the firm still wants to fire the client, it can do so with less political flack.

- **Refer it out.** Refer the client to a smaller law firm. Set up a referral relationship and explain to the client that they will be charged less and get better service from the smaller firm.

- **Cut out small clients at the source.** Change client acceptance procedures to eliminate small matters. Prohibit acceptance of work that particularly attracts individuals and small clients. If the firm must accept some individual work, establish a fixed fee minimum for individual services such as will preparation or residential real estate closings (and make it pretty high).

- **Track and publicize the statistics.** Make a point of publishing a list of client billings by billing attorney every month. The attorneys who constantly maintain a stable of small clients will become obvious. Track at the value of the firm's average and median client in terms of annual revenue. Publish the ratio of clients paying over $100,000 in the last year to the number of partners. If that ratio is less than 3 to 1, the firm's partners are focusing on the wrong kind of practice.

Improving profitability is tough. For most firms, culling small clients represents a relatively easy first step.

"The major difference between a thing that might go wrong and a thing that cannot possibly go wrong is that when a thing that cannot possibly go wrong goes wrong it usually turns out to be impossible to get at or repair."

Douglas Adams, Mostly Harmless

H. Edward Wesemann

Ten Terrible Truths About Law Firm Strategic Planning

It is difficult to find a law firm of any size that has not made some attempt at strategic planning. Indeed, most law firms have devoted hundreds of hours of partner time and thousands of dollars for consultants in strategic planning efforts. Yet, when viewed in the cold light of actual accomplishments, it seems that few firms would rate the strategic planning process as truly successful in accomplishing the firm's objectives.

Why has the process of strategic planning, which has been the subject of such universal acclaim, been so comparatively unsuccessful in many law firms? I believe there are ten inescapable truths about law firms' approach to strategic planning that make the process harder and less rewarding than it should be.

1. **Law firms often have trouble agreeing on their core business objectives.** It sounds silly to say a law firm doesn't know why it is in business, yet many law firms struggle with this core issue. In any

business the primary objective is to increase shareholder value. But when the shareholders all come to work at the business everyday, a whole new set of cultural values comes into play which may or may not be compatible with profit objectives.

If a firm's culture espouses the willingness to do anything, including the subservience of all family and personal interests in the ruthless pursuit of profit, strategic planning is easy. It is equally easy if a firm places collegiality, professional standards and ethics, family and avocations as its foremost objectives, and profit, if any, is viewed as a pleasant by-product. Few, if any law firms are so polarized in their perspective. Instead, the objective of most firms is an acceptable mix of profit and culture. For some firms with a homogeneous partnership and a well established culture, this may not even be an issue. But for most firms, without coming to grips with this mix, it is virtually impossible to do any form of effective strategic planning.

2. **Strategic planning is not a democratic process.** Strategic planning is all about defining a vision and creating a road map to realize that vision. Vision is a function of leadership and, therefore, strategic planning is by its nature a top-down, management driven process. The leader (or a small group of leaders) of the organization, after seeking reasonable counsel and input from as many sources as possible, makes the critical decisions about what the organization wants to do and the basic strategies necessary to accomplish those objectives. Then the leader turns to his or her management team and says "Okay, how are we going to accomplish this."

Law firms turn this upside down. Most law firms aspire to be democratic inclusive organizations. They create large strategic planning committees, carefully designed to have a representative number of members from all offices, practice areas, genders, races and any other stratification they can conceive. It is usually a group so diverse in opinion and agenda that, by their make up, any plan on which they can achieve consensus will be either sufficiently vague to cover all view points or so fragmented as to be self-defeating. Can you picture Jack Walsh at General Electric putting together a strategic planning committee of engineers, production foremen, union representatives, and managers from every product line and asking them to determine GE's strategic objectives?

3. **Mission statements are a waste of energy and enthusiasm.** Without question, mission statements have a value in strategic planning to the extent that they clarify the firm's objectives and values. But too many law firms spend dozens of committee hours trying to draft the definitive aspirational mission statement and, when they finish, publish the statement and think they have accomplished something. In most cases, what they have accomplished is to sap the energy and enthusiasm of the participants for the process with what turns into a meaningless exercise.

It would be far better for the group, or better yet, a couple of firm leaders, to spend half an hour picking five or six statements that represent the firm's core values and vision, especially as they deal with the issues of culture and those things they are not willing to sacrifice to achieve increased profits.

4. **Strategies and tactics are confused.** It is both the beauty and the curse of the lawyer mind that it constantly wants to identify the next action step. For this reason lawyers usually want to skip discussion of strategies and move immediately to tactics.

The strategic planning process is a disciplined way of thinking about planning which forces the planners to consider the optional means of achieving an objective. For example, early on in a strategic process it would not be unusual for some one to suggest that a good profitability strategy would be to open a Paris office. If a firm's strategy is to increase revenues from existing clients and their clients have significant interests in Europe, then a tactic might be to open a Paris office. But to immediately jump to opening an office without going through the process of clarifying the strategy often leads law firms down dangerous and expensive paths.

5. **Planning involves precluding options.** Lawyers, especially business lawyers, are in the business of maintaining options for their clients and they bring that mindset to the strategic planning process. But often the truest measure of the success of a plan's implementation is not what the firm does but what it decides not to do.

The simple logic is that any business has a finite amount of resources to bring to bear on their plan. Resources involve not only money but include management time available and sometimes even such abstract issues as the amount of change that partners can tolerate and the amount of "political capital" the firm's management has available to implement initiatives. To use those resources to take advantage of "unforeseen opportunities" means that, by definition, fewer resources are available to implement the plan.

Does that mean that the plan can never be changed to take advantage of opportunities? Of course not. But, the firm must recognize that diversions from the plan sap resources and, therefore, the benefit of the diversion must be weighed against the risk of not fully implementing the plan.

6. **Too much planning effort is spent worrying about compensation.** Law firms often spend more time debating who will get the spoils if the plan succeeds than implementing the plan. Indeed more than one firm has never gotten around to completing a plan because they got mired in compensation discussions. Appropriate incentives and rewards are important, but the purpose of a strategic plan is to increase the size of the whole pie, not worry about who gets what piece.

7. **The obvious is often overlooked.** Strategic plans often get so involved in sexy issues of new offices and exotic practice areas that they overlook obvious problems. The basic blocking and tackling of law firm profitability improvement is serving clients with good work, working hard, charging appropriate fees, watching costs, maintaining necessary leverage and all the other issues covered in Law Firm Management 101. The first step in any strategic planning process should be a self appraisal of how a firm is doing on the basics.

8. **No one is accountable for implementing the plan.** In order to implement a plan, managers need the authority to manage. Management involves getting people to do things that they don't do on their own and at some point in the implementation of a plan, managers need the authority to compel people to take action.

This means that partners must be accountable to a firm's managers and ultimately to their partners for taking the actions necessary to implement the plan. This is a tough concept for law firms because many partners view themselves as individual professionals whose only responsibility is to their clients. They believe that if the firm decides to do something they disagree with they can simply not participate. But accountability means that all members of the firm are responsible for implementing the plan. No one is allowed to "opt out." It also means that if people do not meet the standards and actions required of them, there are consequences. If a law firm has problems getting partners to submit their time charges promptly or get their bills out, it should come as no surprise that the firm can't get a plan implemented.

9. **Plans are too aggressive.** Once bitten by the strategic planning bug, some firms attempt to implement so many diverse strategies that if every partner devoted their full time efforts to implementation for five years, the objectives could not be achieved. Aiming high is one thing, but a firm only has so many resources.

10. **Objectives are not measurable.** The test of a strategic plan's objectives is whether the firm can look at the plan a year or two later and determine whether they have accomplished anything. Unfortunately objectives such as "improve the quality of our client base" are meaningless if the firm doesn't define what represents a quality client and create a metric to measure comparative quality over time.

Having said all this, law firms are unique entities in which a corporate style of management, much less strategic planning, may not be realistic. Law firms must operate in the environment of what is culturally and politically possible. But, to the extent that a firm can avoid even a few of these "terrible truths," the likelihood of producing a plan that can be implemented will be tremendously enhanced.

"Any organization is like a septic tank. The really big chunks rise to the top."

John Imhoff

"The key to being a good manager is keeping the people who hate me away from those who are still undecided."

Casey Stengel

H. Edward Wesemann

Valuing Managers

Certain management functions must be performed to make any business succeed. If two lawyers start a firm, it is logical that they initially perform these functions themselves. As the firm grows, it may become prudent to hire staff to handle administrative matters. But the core leadership functions of planning, motivating and directing remain with the owners. If the firm gets so large that its diversity and geographic dispersion make it impossible for one or two partners to lead effectively, the firm may delegate some of the leadership functions along logical organization lines, such as by practice group.

In most law firms, large pools of partners are not vying for these management positions. The title of practice group leader may be bestowed on the partner with the largest portfolio of business. Or it may be given to the partner with the lowest billable hours on the theory that if the lawyer can't find anything more worthwhile to do, he or she may as well manage. Most often, though, the position goes to the partner who is willing to step forward and take the job.

A Place for Volunteers?

There are two strikes against the volunteer manager model. The first is a lack of accountability. If a partner performs management functions poorly or, more likely, fails to perform them in more than a cursory manner, little can be done because, in the firm's view, the person is "just a volunteer." More likely than not, there is no one waiting in the wings to take the ineffective manager's place.

Second, the volunteer manager is not part of any line of authority, nor is the manager held accountable. For management to work, the lawyers and staff in the group must recognize the manager's authority. Some exceptional managers can engender this authority through charisma or respect for their accomplishments. But a manager's authority will only be recognized if those who are managed believe there is a formal means to enforce authority through firing, influencing compensation or positively or negatively affecting their work life. By the same token, the manager can't be held accountable if the manager's boss has no formal authority. Consider, for example the practice group leader who reports to the managing partner or the management committee but whose compensation is set by an entirely different committee.

To break this circle, managers must have the authority to function—and be willing to use that authority. But that will not happen as long as managers are viewed by the other partners and themselves as "volunteers." As long as they are not being paid to manage, they are, by definition, volunteers.

You Pay for What You Get

It appears that in many law firms the partnership is unwilling to pay for management. What the partners are unwilling to pay for is, in fact, the *lack* of management. If the only management model they have experienced is "volunteer management" and it has been largely ineffective, the partners' rational reaction is, "Why pay for what I now get for free?"

But what if partners were presented with a different model in which their economic interests were enhanced by paying for management? Indeed, if partners were guaranteed that their compensation would increase through management's efforts, there would be little question about paying for it.

Convincing the partners to pay for management may be easier than convincing the partner-managers that they are being paid to manage. The reasons that law firm partner-managers are willing to provide their time and talents in a volunteer capacity are as varied as their individual motivational constructs. But we know that there is one core constraint on people's willingness to serve in these capacities. That is, if being a manager threatens the individual's financial security. The best response to this concern is three fold.

1. Managers should not have to jeopardize compensation they would otherwise receive if they continued to devote 100 percent of their work time to practicing.

2. Managers should be offered a path for increased compensation — a path that rivals the money they could expect if they continued practicing full time.

3. Managers should have protection when they leave management and return to full time practice.

If managers believe they are primarily paid to practice law under the firm's normal compensation system, they will only perform management tasks to the extent that they do not interfere with their practice activities. Yes, they will approve paperwork and attend meetings. But given the choice of performing a self-initiated task like coaching a member of their group or taking a deposition, they will opt for the revenue-producing activity. They must believe their management tasks are valued at least equally to their practice activities.

Sending the Right Message

The basic compensation of a partner-manager should clearly reflect the value the firm places on the partner's management. However, most firms base compensation on the individual's traditional level of performance—with a few units added for performing a management function. This sends a confusing message.

For example, suppose that Barbara, who has a multimillion-dollar practice and has been one of the firm's highest paid partners, agrees to lead the firm's real estate practice group. Jeff, who has been more of a service partner with a much smaller practice and is paid half as much as Barbara, agrees to take over the corporate practice group. Both are tasked with aggressive growth goals for their groups and asked to devote significant time to their management efforts. So, what is the message we send to these managers? If Barbara cuts back her practice activities and, through her efforts, the real estate practice group grows and prospers, will she get more or less compensation? What about Jeff? Can he ever achieve Barbara's level by virtue of his management activities? Or would this require him to devote more effort to his practice?

The answer to this conundrum lies in the structure of the compensation system we build for our managers. It must integrate both the practice and management sides of the partner's responsibilities and be reasonably individualized to the specifics of each manager's situation. To accomplish this, firms need to manage the activities of each manager by laying out specific expectations. This means, by way of example, saying the following to Jeff:

> *We believe the effective management of the corporate practice group should require about two thirds of your time. To justify your current compensation, you need to have x minimum dollars in billing and working performance (presumably reduced from his current level). If you do this, your compensation will remain the same. If you maintain your personal statistics and your group exceeds its goals, an increase in compensation may be considered. If you meet the minimum expectations for the group and exceed your personal practice performance requirements, you may be eligible for increased compensation but not as large an increase as had the group exceeded its goals. But if you want to continue as a manager, failing to meet your group goals by devoting your efforts to your practice is not an acceptable option.*

For Barbara, it may be necessary to tell her she is too valuable at her current performance level and compensation to perform a management function. This is not to undervalue the importance of management. Everyone has their highest and best use. For some partners, success as a working and billing lawyer may simply price them out of a fair value for management.

Philosophical Questions

The goals that a firm sets for its managers raise philosophical questions: Does the firm want to pay for actions or results? Assume, for example, that a practice group leader is responsible for a list of 10 things (such as conducting a number of client seminars, recruiting a lateral partner in some specialized area, and holding joint meetings with another practice group). Suppose the leader performs all 10 admirably, but the financial performance of the group deteriorates. How will the performance be viewed? Conversely, what if the practice group leader does nothing and through sheer happenstance the group prospers?

The only way group goals can be used to measure the performance of its leader is by a combination of the predetermined plan's execution and the results that occur. That is, a practice group leader should —at least in the short term—be neither penalized nor rewarded if the leader faithfully executes the plan and nothing happens. By the same token, the manager should not be rewarded if there is failure to fulfill the requirements of the plan and through luck the group prospers. The message to the manager is if you execute on what you say you are going to do and results occur, you will get credit for those results.

Providing an Out: Protecting Partners Who Manage

If we expect successful partners to aspire to management, and in the process give up a portion of their practice, there must be a graceful way of easing them back into their practice if they leave management. In essence, we need to provide them with a predetermined parachute. There are three reasons for setting up such protection.

- First, without protection, we create one more disincentive for our brightest and best to contribute their efforts to the firm's betterment.
- Second, it is the fair thing to do and, in most firms, would probably occur even if there was not an established protection.
- Most importantly, holding business unit managers accountable for their performance as managers means that they must be subject to removal if they fail to perform.

Uncertainty about their compensation would only serve to make such decisions more difficult to the detriment of the organization. In fairness, however, the firm does not want to make this protection too generous and thereby create less of an incentive to succeed.

One common way to provide protection is through a formula. For example, the compensation for a partner leaving management will not be decreased for a period of one year for each year spent in management, to a maximum of perhaps four years.

Well-Managed vs. Something Haphazard

It is inconceivable that a multimillion-dollar business would allow itself to be managed by shareholder volunteers who are not paid for the effort. It is hard to argue with the concept that something that is well managed will usually turn out better than something that is allowed to occur haphazardly.

If a law firm wants good management, and believes that it's best to tap the management talents of its partners, then it must develop a parallel career track that rewards partners who are successful. The precise mechanics of how to compensate partner-managers will, of course, be unique to each law firm. What matters most is that the firm clearly states its expectations of managers, and then pays them for meeting or exceeding, those expectations.

"Everywhere is walking distance if you have the time."

Steven Wright

H. Edward Wesemann

Taking the Easy Way Out: Non-Equity Partnerships

Among the most perplexing problems facing many law firms are what to do with associates who do not meet the standards for equity partnership, and what to do with those existing equity partners who are deemed to be less than fully productive. In an attempt to reduce the angst involved in resolving these problems, some law firms have created a new use for the non-equity partner class, and in doing so have created a new partnership action: "de-equitization." The question firms need to face is whether the use of non-equity partnerships as a place to park attorneys who do not meet the standards for equity partnership is a politically easy but ineffective solution to a difficult problem.

Non-equity partnerships have become increasing popular with law firms as an alternative partnership tier, both for the promotion of associates and as a form of "limbo" for lateral- entry attorneys.

For associates, the jump from being an employee to becoming an owner represents much more than a change in title. In most firms, the measure of associates' success, indeed, the basis for promotion to partner, is heavily weighted on their performance as working attorneys. Associate compensation is largely based on the marketplace: There is rarely much difference in compensation among similarly sized firms within a city. But when an associate is promoted to partner, compensation has nothing to do with the marketplace; instead, it's dependent on how profitable the firm is (the size of the pie) and how each partner compares with the others (the size of each partner's slice of the pie).

"Two tier" firms, those that have an intervening non-equity step for new partners, are able to take some of the economic pressure off associates for a period of time as they adjust to their business development and client management responsibilities. In some firms, non-equity status may also help associates move from the certainty of a monthly paycheck to the inconsistency of being paid out of profits.

For lateral-entry attorneys, non-equity partnership allows firms to substantiate portable billings, work ethic, and cultural compatibility before vesting them with the tenure that generally comes with equity partnership. Often, it also allows the firm to structure a compensation deal that protects the firm from overpaying the lateral attorney in the event that he or she is less successful than anticipated.

The role of the non-equity partner varies tremendously among firms. In some firms, there is little difference between equity and non-equity partners: The non-equity partner enjoys all of the privileges of partnership, including the right to attend partnership meetings, receive financial reports, vote in partnership affairs, and in all ways holds him- or herself out as a partner. In other firms, non-equity partners are viewed as advanced-level associates with few, if any, trappings of partnership. Until now, few firms have spent time fretting about documenting what it means to be a non-equity partner because it was only meant to be a transitionary classification.

New Uses

But new uses of the non-equity status may significantly change the structure of law firms. Traditionally, associates have joined firms with the hope that, after some unspecified number of years, they will be able to reach for the brass ring and, perhaps, be elected to partnership. Usually, few specifics are given to the associates about the standards on which partnership decisions are made, how much capital contribution is required of a new partner, or even how much money they will earn as a partner. Associates who are not elected have been expected to fall on their swords and seek their fortunes elsewhere, under the policy of "up or out."

Some firms are finding, however, that the new realities of associate profitability and ambitions are rendering this model antiquated. Firms that take the time to do the math are finding that their most profitable fee-earners are senior associates and young partners. At their level of sophistication, lawyers with eight to ten or so years of experience command high hourly rates, rack up a large number of hours, and earn (comparatively) low compensation. The last thing a successful firm wants to do is lose its most profitable timekeepers to an up-or-out policy.

At the same time, some law firms are experiencing a new phenomenon -- associates turning down offers of equity partnership. Having become comfortable in their practices, some associates look to the prospect of becoming a partner and, instead of a brass ring, see only the pressure to generate new business for the firm and sign on for a big capital account loan just when they've paid off their law school bills. That's in addition to paying their own employee benefit costs and a larger Social Security contribution, and waiting for large chunks of their compensation until year-end.

Although there is a strong desire to present themselves to the world (not to mention their mothers and spouses) as partners in the firm, the relative security of associateship has a certain appeal to it. For both the firm and the associate, therefore, non-equity partnership may be an attractive alternative to the traditional equity partner status.

De-equitization of Partners

At the other end of the spectrum is the problem that law firms have with equity partners who either never raised themselves to the level of partnership expectations or who have partially retired without telling anyone. This was not a problem until about 20 years ago because firms were "big tents" that could

27

accommodate a wide variety of work levels through compensation systems that reflected differing levels of effort and financial performance.

In the early 1980s, however, *The American Lawyer* magazine popularized a new statistic as the measure of law firm economic success - profits per equity partner. With the public availability of law firms' comparative financial information, profits per partner developed into a competitive issue. Lateral prospects used PPP as a means of differentiating among firms; it became the first cut for judging the suitability of law firms as merger partners. Even within law firms, average PPP statistics became as important to individual partners as their own actual compensation in evaluating their firm's performance.

It didn't take long for firms to realize that the denominator in this calculation (the number of partners) is as important as the level of profits themselves. Indeed, by adjusting the partnership ranks and converting equity partners to some other status, a firm could see a double-digit increase in its average profits without bringing in one more dime in revenue or cutting a single expense.

Taking the Easy Way Out

The biggest problem with the use of non-equity partnerships is that it makes decisions too easy. Advising a likable associate that he or she has been elected to non-equity partnership is certainly a less onerous task than telling them they have been rejected for equity partnership and must either remain an associate or leave the firm. Unfortunately, some firms are finding that what is relatively painless in the short term can have devastating long-term ramifications.

Associates promoted to non-equity partner status --to keep them onboard without letting them share in the profits-- may be strung along by the hope of full equity partnership, when in actuality they have already been deemed to be lacking in the qualities for equity partnership. Caught in this amorphous system, they may even be reconsidered for equity partnership year after year, particularly if they have a protector within the partnership. Some candidates, due to sheer longevity of their appearance on consideration reports, might actually be elected to equity partnership in a year when the recommending committee is feeling particularly soft-hearted. As firms now attempt to deal with unproductive partners, they often realize that it is just such "lapses" in their partnership admission process that caused the problem in the first place.

By the same token, using de-equitization to deal with underproductive partners is certainly easier than firing the person. But from a practical point of view, this step rarely resolves the underlying issues for either the firm or the newly demoted partner. In fact, the more likely outcome is that, rather than sending a "wake-up call" to the partner, his or her reaction will be a declining sense of urgency. This often shows up in a lack of responsiveness and a deteriorating client-service ethic. It doesn't take long for this decline to be recognized by the partners assigning work and, given the alternative of using senior associates with a comparable skill level and a more responsive attitude, the demoted partner's hours soon dry up. All of these factors combine to sabotage hopes of returning to being a fully productive member of the firm, or ever regaining full-equity status.

Worse, because non-equity partners fall between senior associates and equity partners in their level of practice sophistication, if a non-equity partner attracts work that would be valued by up-and-coming senior associates, an important associate development opportunity is missed. Good associates are able to see handwriting on the wall very quickly and, rather than risk being passed over for partnership themselves, will seek better learning opportunities at competing firms.

Perhaps most important, rarely do law firms want to be judged on the basis of people they reject for, or remove from, equity partnership. But the outside world, and often even associates and employees within the firm, cannot distinguish between equity partners and non-equity partners. If the individual doesn't meet the firm's standards for equity partnership, then including him or her as a partner devalues the designation for those who do meet the standard.

No Silver Bullets

Not surprisingly, there is no easy way to deal with difficult personnel decisions. There may be legitimate situations where time spent as a non-equity partner may help an associate mature into a successful partner. There may also be situations where being reclassified from equity partner to non-equity partner status does provide a "wake-up call" for a partner that compensation adjustments alone could not. But the truth is that those exceptions are few and far between. Being reclassified to non-equity partner status will likely only exacerbate whatever deficiencies were previously evident in the demoted attorney's work.

Increasingly, law firms are utilizing non-equity partnership status to avoid the tough decisions; some have amended their partnership agreements to make it procedurally easier to create non-equity partners. This is akin to removing the salary caps for sports team owners -- it facilitates bad decisions. If non-equity partnerships offer management an easy course of action, then there must be a supervising authority who can throw up a red flag occasionally. Making a partnership vote a requirement for promoting or demoting current attorneys to non-equity partnership may make the process a little less convenient, but years from now when someone asks "How did this guy become a partner?" or "Why is this person still a partner?," the answer will not be "Because the firm took the easy way out."

"I have enough money to last me the rest of my life, unless I buy something."

Jackie Mason

H. Edward Wesemann

Ten Terrible Truths about Partner Compensation Systems

It seems that sole practitioners are about the only lawyers who don't devote a significant amount of time and energy talking about compensation. In virtually every other firm, regardless of whether it has 5 lawyers or 500, partners spend more time talking about each other's compensation than any other management topic. In fact, it is rare that any meeting or retreat of a law firm partnership doesn't dissolve into a discussion of the inadequacies of the compensation system. Law firm partners love nothing more than fretting about how they pay each other.

Given the per partner profits many firms enjoy, it wouldn't seem that dividing the spoils should be such a demanding task. Yet in some firms committees devote hundreds of hours to delving through reams of computer reports in search of the perfect allocation of the firm's net income. I believe there are 10 inescapable truths about law firms' approach to compensating their partners that make the process harder and less successful than it should be.

1. **Lawyers often equate *compensation* with *management*.** It is not

surprising that the public views lawyers as people who are only motivated by money; because that is precisely the way lawyers view themselves and their partners. "You get what you pay for" is the mantra of most law firm managers and, as a result, there is the belief that if you just set the reward high enough, lawyers will do whatever is asked of them. That may work with commission sales people but few lawyers share the mercenary psychological makeup of encyclopedia salesmen. And, if it really is all about money, a firm shouldn't be surprised when its biggest rainmaker moves to the firm across the street for more money.

2. **Law firms believe in** *Theory X.* Management theorists suggest that there are two schools of thought on motivation. *Theory X* postulates that everyone is naturally indolent and, if given the chance, will goof off on the job. *Theory Y* suggests that people actually want to work hard and do a good job, but management must motivate and train them. Law firms are hard line *Theory X* so there is a lot of concern about what happens if a partner stops working or loses his or her billing base. As a result most partner compensation systems are designed to assure that no one is overpaid.

3. **Management is divorced from compensation.** Law firms expect their management to accomplish tasks. They also make compensation the primary motivational device for rewarding accomplishment or penalizing failure. Yet, in many firms partner compensation is decided by a committee, which is separate from its management. Worse, even many of the largest law firms with hundreds of millions of dollars in revenues are run by part time managers whose compensation is based more on the clients they originate or their billable hours than on the success of their management efforts.

4. **Partners are constantly afraid of being cheated.** Unlike virtually every other business, most law firms have open compensation systems where every partner knows the compensation of every other partner. As a result, partners are more concerned about how they are being paid in relation to their fellow partners than the actual amount of their compensation. Reward can be more political than motivational.

5. **There are no ties between compensation and the performance it is designed to incent.** In many firms the compensation list is

published in a memo with no mention of why individual partners' pay is being increased or deceased. Firms rarely announce their expectations of partners, either as a group or individually. Instead, they give out vague signals on what is the expected behavior or level of performance.

6. **Committees avoid responsibility for compensation actions.** Typically, partner compensation is set by a compensation committee so individual members can deflect responsibility for the results. In many firms, the compensation procedures keep the proceedings of the committee secret to assure that no partner can fully understand or question the message transmitted by compensation actions.

7. **Compensation systems ignore motivation.** Psychologists tell us that recognition is, for most people, one of the greatest motivational tools that managers have. Most businesses that want their people to be successful look for every opportunity to hand out awards, send the best people on trips or give dinners in their honor. Lawyers are generally thought of as having high ego needs, yet law firms usually seem to strive to avoid singling anyone out for praise. Shouldn't bonus checks be handed out at a gala black-tie dinner?

8. **Law firms drive partners to be more interested in the size of their slice rather than the size of the pie.** Increasing a partner's share of profits is a zero sum game. For one partner's share to go up, another's must go down. Unfortunately, many firms spend more time *dividing* than *creating*. It would seem to make more sense to focus partners' interest on increasing the total profits of the firm.

9. **There are not enough dollars to reward some things that really matter.** By becoming meritocracies, law firms have embarked along a system of devoting a disproportionately large share of profits to the superstars who control business. As a result, there is little left to differentiate the rewards to those partners whose contributions (mentor associates, performing pro bono work, bar activities) create the culture of the firm and define the profession.

10. **Many of the most profitable law firms have lockstep compensation systems.** Since compensation systems are highly confidential aspects of law firm governance, it is difficult to be definitive. However, there is at least anecdotal evidence to suggest that there is a correlation

between profitability and compensation systems. Firms with the highest per partner profits seem to have more subjective ways of determining partner compensation, including lockstep or modified lockstep systems (systems where increases in compensation are heavily determined by seniority). Less profitable firms seem to depend more on formulas and other objective statistics.

The real truth for law firms is that **three years of law school doesn't supercede five million years of evolution.** Nothing about being a lawyer causes a partner to be motivated by anything different than doctors, business executives, plumbers or bus drivers. Therefore, law firms should look outside their profession when designing compensation and recognition systems. It could have amazing results.

"Abbott: Now, on the St. Louis team we have Who's on first, What's on second, I Don't Know is on third.
Costello: That's what I want to find out."

Bud Abbott and Lou Costello

H. Edward Wesemann

Breaking the Wall: Six Rules to Managing The Three Million Dollar Practice and Beyond

It is relatively rare to find a major business developer in a law firm who maintains a truly large practice. Certainly there are situations where a partner is the responsible attorney for a large corporate relationship that may involve $10 or $15 million in billings. There are situations where, by virtue of a relationship with senior management, an attorney may be the lynchpin for a total corporate relationship worth millions of dollars. But, typically, mega books of business are more the result of the rules of the firm's compensation system than actual client responsibility.

It seems that most law firm rainmakers seem to hit a wall when their billings hit a certain level, usually at about the three million mark. They have gotten to this level through hard work and paying extraordinary attention to the needs of their clients. To advance beyond this level, rainmakers find that they have to depend more greatly on other attorneys to maintain their client relationships – and that's where it all falls apart.

There are, however, some lawyers who have broken through the wall and seem to be able to manage virtually a limitless number of relationships totally well into the eight figures. Indeed, we have a client who year in and year out maintains a billing base of more than $10 million. The clients may change but the total size of the portfolio continues to grow each year. What's more, the average client pays less than $300,000 annually in fees.

I recently set about learning how this attorney accomplishes what so few lawyers can do (for purposes of confidentiality I'll call the attorney Joe Smith but I assure you that he is a real person). I talked to him and some of his partners and associates and came away with six rules that seem to work extraordinarily well for him.

Rule #1: The client must believe that Mr. Smith is an active part of every engagement

No client wants to feel like they are getting the second string. Yet, Mr. Smith can't attend every meeting and be involved in every phone call. The answer is to have well trained associates who make a point of dropping Mr. Smith's name several times in every conversation – "Joe asked me to call and give you an update on the Jones matter" or "I'm meeting with Joe on this issue later today and he asked me to give you an advanced briefing." A primary task of every attorney working for Mr. Smith is to constantly put a specific spin on communications. That spin should make the client believe that the only reason they are talking to the associate is because Mr. Smith is too busy working on their stuff to be involved in the conversation. But a primary rule and a firing offense is to ever lie to the client about Mr. Smith's involvement.

To make this work, two things must occur. First, the associates must be willing to put aside their egos and work for Joe's benefit. This is accomplished by paying above average compensation, generous bonuses tied to the retention of the clients they are working with and handoffs of billing responsibility for matters for Joe's clients that are too small for him to take an interest in. Second, Mr. Smith must really know what is going on with his clients. That's accomplished by rule #2…

Rule #2: There is a mandatory attendance early every morning of everyone working on a Joe Smith matter.

Taken right out of the pages of LA Law, every day begins by going around the table and talking about what was accomplished yesterday and what is going to be accomplished today. The focus is not on process. Instead they talk about accomplishments. Mr. Smith takes notes and frequently asks probing questions about why more has not been accomplished or about a matter that has not been mentioned. One associate describes it as being akin to hospital rounds for interns in a teaching hospital. Mr. Smith uses the sessions for enhancing the legal skills of the group by learning from one another, to publicly recognize extraordinary accomplishment and, upon occasion to humiliate unsatisfactory performance. But the primary purpose is to facilitate rule #3…

Rule #3: Mr. Smith talks to every client at least every week and much more often when a matter is highly active.

Joe Smith views his role as the conductor of an orchestra. He selects the music and the venue, helps market and publicize the performances and directs who plays what notes, when. But the conductor never actually plays any music himself. By the same token, Mr. Smith virtually never does any actual legal work. His day is taken up in conversation with clients, advising attorneys working on his matters during dozens of short conversations during each day and calling or taking calls from clients. In fact, one of his two administrative assistances does virtually nothing but manage his phone traffic. Joe is not afraid to leave detailed voice mail messages but he never uses e-mail. He believes strongly that "they need to hear my voice."

Joe is meticulous about keeping track of his time at quarter hour increments even for clients where he has a fixed fee or retainer relationship (which is most of his clients). His assistant records every call he is on and every person who comes into his office.

To create a purpose for Mr. Smith's client communication calls, he has rule #4…

Rule 4: Every client must have some specific next expected action that will be happening within 7 to 10 days

Joe Smith believes that client relationships languish and clients are lost when the intensity of the relationship dwindles. One of the things that is communicated in the daily meeting is the next action step. It may be something that is due to the client or it may be something for which the client has responsibility. In some cases the action step may be pretty flimsy but it establishes a justification for Mr. Smith to make contact with the client. And, it never causes the client to wonder what is going on with their matter.

Of course, the reason for Mr. Smith investing so much time in phone contacts is to generate business that meets his rule #5.

Rule #5: Every matter Mr. Smith takes responsibility for must represent a significant financial investment for the client and receive CEO or Board of Directors level attention.

It is amazing to listen to a conversation between Mr. Smith and his client regarding engagement for a matter that does not achieve the standard for acceptance. It goes something like this:

"Thank you for thinking of us for this matter. I'm asking one of my partners, Tom Johnson to take responsibility for it. Tom has my complete confidence. I know that it might be your preference that I handle it but then I wouldn't have the time to work on the especially important matters that you and my other clients have entrusted me with. But, if you are ever dissatisfied by any aspect of our performance or can't get a hold of Tom, please call me immediately."

Mr. Smith then sets up a meeting with the client and Tom. If the client is local, they meet in the client's office. Tom usually attends to make the introduction but excuses himself after about 15 minutes. If the client is out-of-town, Tom will travel to meet with the client and Mr. Smith will attend by phone for the first few minutes. Unless the matter is really small, every engagement begins with a face to face meeting.

It is important to note that the partner, to whom Mr. Smith hands off the matter (it is almost always to a partner level attorney), receives billing and origination credit for the matter in the firm's compensation system as well as any other small matters they can generate from the client. The reason Mr. Smith can hand off a matter for a large client with confidence is his constant stressing to his attorneys of rule #6…

Rule #6: We are offering one level of service – That level must be extraordinary – Clients will not detect a service difference based on the size of the matter

The constant drive of the firm is for greater client service which typically involves responsiveness. The firm's prompt return of phone calls is legendary. Secretaries are trained to say to clients, "I know Mr. Smith always wants to know when you call. Would you like me to interrupt the call he is on or may he call you as soon as he gets off the phone." Every attorney's business card has their home and mobile numbers. Most client meetings take place in the client's office.

* * *

So those are my observations about one lawyer who has broken through the $3 million wall. I'm not sure that any one rule is more or less important than the others or that this prescription will work for any other attorney. The one thing I failed to mention which may contribute to "Mr. Smith's" success is an incredible work ethic and a brutal travel schedule. But I guess working hard and being an excellent lawyer should go without mention

"Careful. We don't want to learn from this."

Calvin and Hobbs

Knowledge Management…
Is the Emperor Wearing Clothes?

Get together a group of law firm managing partners, legal administrators, or law firm IT directors, and you can bet the hot topic of discussion will be "knowledge management."

"KM," as knowledge management is termed among insiders, is the holy grail of law firm information technology. It is the end that finally justifies all of the money firms have poured into technology. KM is viewed as such an important "next step" that at least two managing partners at top firms label it their highest priority for the next couple of years.

Questioning the importance of KM is akin to firing up a cigarette in New York City's mayor's office. Naysayers are quickly booed down with the unassailable justification that clients are demanding formal knowledge management systems from their outside counsel. Therefore, to effectively compete for sophisticated clients, law firms must be able to demonstrate that they can leverage what they have learned in previous engagements to decrease the cost of providing future legal services.

Knowledge management is not a new topic. It began when litigators put together brief banks in file cabinets and corporate attorneys created clause books. With the development of document management software, firms could recall documents by categories, by key words, or by full-text search. The current phase in knowledge management seems to be spearheaded by firms' Chief Information Officers and Technology Committees in an attempt to draw returns on investment from their massive technology outlays.

The most common models for law firm knowledge management come from the large accounting and consulting firms. Ernst & Young, for example, maintains a knowledge management center where over 100 employees are dedicated to receiving daily reports from each of the firm's professionals around the world. The information is codified and entered into a database that can be accessed by E&Y accountants and consultants through on-line portals.

Despite a huge investment in knowledge management by the biggest law firms around the world, and despite supposedly high-priority interest among the largest buyers of legal services, law firms are having a tough time putting together effective KM programs. Large firm legal administrators point to a number of difficulties.

> *1. Lack of Payback.* It is difficult for managing partners and executive committees to push for the capital investment and partner cooperation necessary to implement knowledge management without a demonstrable financial benefit. For firms tied to hourly billing, the results of a successful knowledge management system are less time billed and lower revenues. The benefits of stronger client relationships and competitive advantages are difficult to quantify against million-dollar KM operating budgets and recurring losses in revenue each time the information is used. It's the same old story of revenue needs versus technology-induced efficiency.

> *2. Partner Reluctance.* From the perspective of the partners, a huge part of their value to the firm and its clients is the information they have

acquired over years of practice and which they carry around in their heads. To gratuitously contribute knowledge to a databank where it can be accessed by any firm attorney and, perhaps, by clients directly, removes partners from the direct delivery of their knowledge. It threatens their value to the client and the firm. On balance, most attorneys would conclude that their personal interests are better served by controlling the information themselves. Better, from their point of view, to limit access to situations where they receive the payback.

3. *Lack of Sincere Client Interest.* Few clients have demonstrated sincere interest in KM. While clients may talk a good game, and include a section on knowledge management in their RFP's, they are not, on all but the most routine matters, willing to let their work be anything less than custom-crafted, even though "off the rack" solutions may be available from the knowledge management system. Similarly, many clients seem unenthusiastic about work product for which they paid dearly, but that is also available to other clients through a KM system.

4. *Inability to Enforce Knowledge Management.* A KM system only has value if attorneys routinely input their work product and consult the system when performing work. Law firms that have problems requiring their attorneys to submit time sheets, and to do their billing promptly, are certainly going to find it difficult compelling compliance to a KM policy.

But, perhaps the greatest difficulty with KM is that it is being promulgated as a technology-related initiative. In fact, the IT department may be the last place knowledge management needs to reside. KM is really a practice management tool that ought to reside with professional service managers, not with systems managers.

A February, 2000 article in the *Harvard Business Review*, "What's Your Strategy for Managing Knowledge?" points out that two competing management consulting firms operate vastly different knowledge management systems. Ernst & Young operates a codified system that uses sophisticated computer-search capability to permit any consultant to access any document, form, checklist, or piece of information that has been created on a specific topic.

McKinsey, on the other hand, focuses on directing the inquirer to the person that created the information. The difference is that Ernst & Young's system provides you with the recipe; McKinsey's lets you talk to the chef who created it.

The Ernst & Young system is excellent for repetitive consultative functions, similar to the commodity-level practices that many law firms are attempting to move away from. The McKinsey function provides greater potential for creative and unique engagements, the equivalent of legal work that commands premium billing. The Ernst & Young system requires extensive sophisticated systems and personnel, while McKinsey's way could be done with little more than a rolodex.

For law firms, it is important to note that both approaches provide economic benefit to the consulting firms because they bill by a fixed fee for an engagement rather than at hourly rates, like law firms. That may be an insurmountable challenge for some lawyers.

In any event, the real question for law firms becomes, what is the practice management value of a knowledge management system.

Knowledge management makes all sorts of sense. It is impossible to justify anything less. A law firm with less than maximum technology is just a welfare state. When law firms were smaller and less complex organizations, access to knowledge could take place in hallways, at the water cooler, or over lunch. As global organizations, law firms need to find new means of conveying *knowledge* rather than work product. This need requires an emphasis on communication rather than technology.

The best interests of the client may not be served by having a boilerplate answer to every legal issue stored in a computer. Instead, the big win for a client may be to have access to the broadest selection of attorneys from within a firm, regardless of their office location or practice group.

In the practice of law for sophisticated clients with complex legal matters, knowledge management is the ability to identify and access the very best person in a firm to handle specific aspects of a matter. The client benefits from knowledge management through the quality of the legal work product, and from only paying for the time spent by the most qualified attorney where his or her precise expertise is required.

The hourly rate of this lawyer may be high but few clients balk at paying higher rates for the most qualified person to perform the work, as opposed to paying lower rates for less qualified practitioners who bill more time, and often higher total fees, to produce an inferior result.

For the law firm, the concept of knowledge management as a practice management tool gets it past the age-old problem of fewer hours billed as efficiency increases. A KM system that accesses the best attorney, rather than a boilerplate legal product, is tailor-made for a firm that is migrating upward, away from commodity and toward premium legal work.

That's why it is so important for such firms not to get diverted to technology systems designed for commodity practice.

How It's Done

There are a variety of ways to implement knowledge management that may or may not require a computer.

One simple way is by creating a *Knowledge Concierge*. The Knowledge Concierge tracks which lawyers have worked on what issues. Their sources of information can be as simple as new matter reports and telephone conversations with attorneys recorded in relatively unsophisticated databases. An attorney seeking guidance on a client issue would be referred to the available attorney with the best and most applicable knowledge and experience. At lots of firms, being the Knowledge Concierge is the primary job of the practice group chairs.

Another means several firms use to implement knowledge management is a weekly *"Learnings"* report. Each attorney distributes a weekly report to the practice group chair that outlines the most important things the attorney has done in the past week and what he or she has learned in the process. "Learnings" may be unique facets of the law or an industry, a legal process, or even industry gossip. A designated paralegal prepares a "highlights" email that goes to every lawyer in the practice group and is input in a section of the document management system where it can be full-text searched.

To be effective, a knowledge management system must meet the needs of the lawyers, their clients, and the firm in a manner that removes the disincentives for participation and support by all three. As a result:

- Clients get access to the best talent available to work on their issues without paying for educational time or unnecessary research. The client pays a premium rate in return for unique knowledge and efficiently produced work product.

- Lawyers with special experience or expertise get to work on the most sophisticated projects in their area, enhance their knowledge and experience level, and charge time at premium rates for their efforts. They don't feel cheated because they've been technologically disinherited from their own expertise.

- The cost implications of this kind of knowledge management are minimal. Even in the largest firms, it involves the part-time efforts of a few people. The payback is the generation of premium rate work and client satisfaction.

There will, undoubtedly, be continuous new knowledge management iterations for years into the future. The end result may, in fact, be a technologically based system.

But until we have the institutional ability to consistently move the thought processes and memories of our best and brightest attorneys into databases, and the technology to get that data out again as equally meaningful information, IT-based knowledge management systems will only help law firms perform their least profitable work less profitably.

"Never eat more than you can lift."

Miss Piggy

H. Edward Wesemann

Pricing to the Market

I have the privilege of speaking at and facilitating a goodly number of law firm retreats and I enjoy having the opportunity to pick the brains of partners who are otherwise not involved in firm management. For the past few months, at every law firm retreat or legal conference I facilitated, I posed the question, "How do you establish your firm's billing rates?" Most commonly, partners always answered, "We charge what the market will bear."

That seems like a rather vague sentiment though. Just how does a law firm know what the market will bear? I know one managing partner who believes in the "gag threshold" method. That is, when a client opens a bill, the dollar amount should be high enough to cause the constricting of throat muscles, but not so high to cause the bill to get tossed in the trash. Indeed, for many firms, judging what the market will bear involves a game of brinksmanship -- the firm raises rates until the client screams or, in the worst case, takes their legal work elsewhere.

As an alternative, lawyers could simply ask clients how much they're willing to pay. But that typically doesn't work out well – not so much because the client lies (although the question begs for a low ball answer), but because most clients are simply unaware of how much they're willing to pay. As the last cottage industry left in America, law firms continue to customize services in a manner that makes it nearly impossible for any but the most astute client to compare prices among competitors. Not surprisingly, the result is often a level of sticker shock for the client that reaches or surpasses that "gag threshold."

For the law firm, all of this adds up to inefficient market pricing. That is, because firms lack any effective means of measuring the acceptable client price, they consistently fall prey to overcharging in weak markets and undercharging in strong markets. When a firm charges more than a client is willing to pay, the client will either complain or take their business elsewhere. In either case, the firm is offered immediate feedback of their price being too high. No such feedback exists when the price is too low. Most law firms, being the risk-averse organizations they are, safely react to this situation by preferring to charge too little, thereby avoiding the risk of offending or losing a client.

Worse, many lawyers routinely train clients to seek discounted fees. Most law firms have established a standard billing rate for each attorney (equivalent to the manufacturer's recommended price for a product). At many firms though, partners regularly provide clients a discount from this rate, eventually reaching a point where charging "full rates" is a rare accomplishment. Clients are quick to figure out how to play this game.

Price Sensitivity

If law firms intend to charge clients based on what the market will bear, then they need a mechanism for figuring precisely what, in fact, each client is willing to pay. This involves understanding each client's unique circumstances in the marketplace and setting the firm's price in appreciation of those individual circumstances. To do this, firms must first determine the client's level of price sensitivity. To start with, I think there are basically four types of clients, each with their own level of price sensitivity:

<u>Price-Based Clients</u>

There are no purely price-driven clients. All clients understand to some degree that "you get what you pay for," i.e., they recognize some differentiation among the quality of lawyers and legal services. But for the extreme price-sensitive client, the driving consideration in selecting counsel is price. After the completely unqualified lawyers and law firms have been screened, price is what it's all about.

Of course, the best example of the extreme price-sensitive client is the insurance company. Insurance companies are in the business of assessing risk and, clearly, they have determined that above a certain level of quality, the difference among firms in affecting the actual likelihood of a successful outcome is insufficient to justify anything but the lowest possible price.

Extreme price-sensitive clients are easy to spot. Price is the first thing they ask about, and price is the dominant feature of any conversation.

Relationship Clients

At the other polarization of price sensitivity are relationship clients. These are clients who perceive a special relationship with their attorney or law firm. They place such value on that relationship that, as long as they don't believe they're being gouged, they are essentially blind to price. Often the relationship involves a personal bond between the lawyer and client, but it can also involve the client and the firm. For example, when a client hires a preeminent firm or attorney, they are essentially saying, "Look at who is representing me!" They pay to create a relationship where none previously existed.

Relationship clients tend to be sensitive and selective about who in a firm will actually do their work, and they rarely address price as an issue.

Convenience Clients

For these clients, the driving issue is making problems disappear. Convenience may take many forms, ranging from handling a transaction in Santiago with minimum hassle, to defending a TRO at a 9 a.m. Monday morning hearing. Often convenience is a function of urgency. Convenience always involves the client's ability to move a problem away from their desk and onto a lawyer's desk.

Not surprisingly, convenience clients are willing to pay the price for their urgency. They are not price sensitive (but bill them fast because they may be a few months later).

Value-Based Clients

All clients are value-based to some extent. They make rational decisions about pricing based on what they believe they receive in return of their investment. Then they compare this to competing firms in the marketplace. Clients may place value on the level of client service, the success of the outcome, or a variety of other perceptions.

Often value is actually driven by price. Clients have very little information on which to base price decisions. Outside of a commodity-type service that a client may have used before, it is difficult to compare prices or gain insight into what legal services should cost. For this reason, clients may place greater value on expensive services and less value on inexpensive services.

Analyzing Price Sensitivity

Having done a little research on what the market will bear, it seems that 10 significant factors dictate the level of price sensitivity. To understand what to charge a value based client, ask the following:

1. How well does the client know what other law firms charge for the services sought? *(Clients without a point of reference tend to be less price-sensitive.)*

2. How difficult is it for a client to compare fees among competing law firms? *(The more defined the matter and the more routine the service, the greater the fee sensitivity.)*

3. How difficult is it for a client to change law firms? *(The less technically complex the matter, the more price sensitive the client.)*

4. How much importance does the client place on having a high-prestige, big-name firm, and are you such a firm? *(Price-sensitive clients tend not to care about prestige.)*

5. In the scope of the client's legal budget, how significant is this engagement? *(Clients tend to be more price sensitive on smaller, low-profile engagements.)*

6. How important is a successful result to the client? *(Results with little impact on a client's profitability tend to be more price sensitive.)*

7. Where does this engagement fall in the corporate hierarchy? *(Engagements involving board of directors or corporate officer visibility are less price sensitive than projects reporting to people further down the chain of command.)*

8. Who's paying the bill? *(Engagements subject to court or agency review or those where client cost is partially shared by an insurance or other company, tend to be more price sensitive.)*

9. Who initiated your first conversation about fees, the attorney or the client? *(If the client initiates fee conversations or offers a fee agreement, it is a sure sign of high price sensitivity.)*

10. What is the business purpose of the engagement? *(If the objective is to correct or remediate a problem, the client may be more price sensitive than if the result were the accomplishment of a gain.)*

The bottom line is that if a law firm is pricing to what the market will bear, it is necessary that it understand its clients' level of price sensitivity. And, logically, pricing to the market must take advantage of favorable market conditions as well as the unfavorable.

"If I had only known, I would have been a locksmith."

Albert Einstein

A Common Sense Approach to Cross-selling

In many law firms, lawyers who have tried to cross-sell come back saying it is just too hard and they conclude that cross-selling doesn't work. I think a big part of the problem is that we are treating our clients like marketing targets for new business instead of serving them as the trusted advisors they expect us to be.

This may be one of those places where we can learn significant lessons from the big four accounting firms. In Australia and South Africa, where accounting firms offering legal services has become a part of everyday competitive life for law firms, the accountants have become experts in converting simple accounting gigs into expansive professional service engagements. In a corporate transaction, it is not unusual for the accountants (who are usually involved before the attorneys) to simply bring their lawyers along and start parceling out the legal work. If the client objects, the accountants remind the client how much time will be lost and how much duplication will occur if they have to stop and wait for another law firm to get up to speed.

This may be too aggressive and pushy for law firms in the U.S., but let's see what we can learn from the experience.

How not to cross-sell

In a typical cross-selling situation, Larry, a corporate attorney, wants to cross-sell the firm's environmental services to one of his clients. He invites the client to have lunch saying that there is someone he wants the client to meet. Larry invites his partner Mary, an environmental partner, to attend, and the firm's marketing director prepares a briefing paper on the client and a package of material on the firm's environmental practice.

Larry introduces the client to Mary as they are seated at a private downtown dining club where the firm has a membership. They spend the lunch having an enjoyable conversation about baseball, politics, their respective children and the economy. It's a comfortable social lunch and neither Larry nor Mary wants to commercialize it with a sales pitch. When the check comes, Larry realizes that he has stalled long enough and it's time to get down to business. He introduces Mary as an environmental lawyer with the firm and she launches into a five-minute soliloquy on the firm's environmental capability. Mary ends by giving the client a half-pound of marketing material and inviting him to call if he ever needs environmental counsel.

The client walks out of the lunch scratching his head and wondering, "what was that all about?" Larry and Mary give each other a high five on the way back to the office and congratulate themselves on a successful cross-marketing presentation. A year goes by and the client's environmental work continues to go to other law firms. The reaction from Larry and Mary is that cross-selling is a great idea in concept but it just doesn't work in the real world.

Working to improve the relationship rather than sell the client

The firm, through Larry, already has a relationship with the client and, presumably, the client respects Larry's judgment as his corporate attorney. Wouldn't it make more sense to build on that relationship rather than starting from scratch by making, what is in effect, a cold call with Mary? Suppose instead, that Larry and Mary offered an effective demonstration of the firm's understanding of the client's environmental needs – thereby using the occasion to present the client with something of value as part of the firm's on-going client service effort.

Rather than a social lunch, what if Larry invites Mary to participate in a routine meeting with the client on an acquisition they have been working on. In advance of the meeting, Larry briefs Mary on the deal and asks her to do some research on environmental issues that could impact the transaction, focusing on solutions that would decrease environmental liability while permitting the deal to close.

At the meeting, Larry indicates that he was concerned about possible environmental liabilities in the deal so he wanted to get Mary involved. Mary gives a brief presentation, including an outline of the issues that require further review. Perhaps Mary also comments about other environmental issues facing the client suggesting the transaction might provide an opportunity to resolve all of these issues with debt financing. Larry ends the conversation by suggesting that Mary move forward on the issues and meet with the client's operating people. In all likelihood the client will authorize the work and be thankful to Larry for his proactive handling of the problems.

What's happened here?

For the price of one non-billable hour of research time by Mary, Larry has made himself and the firm look good in the eyes of the client and, in all likelihood, picked up a piece of the client's environmental work (in which case the non-billable speculative hour by Mary becomes billable). Now all Mary has to do is provide the client with extraordinary service and demonstrate what a capable environmental attorneys she is.

The simple fact is that attorneys and clients alike feel more comfortable when cross-selling occurs as part of an overall service offering, instead of a stilted marketing effort. And the worst-case scenario is that Mary has lost an hour of time, which isn't that much more money than the cost of a far more difficult cross-selling business lunch.

"Yesterday I was a dog. Today I'm a dog. Tomorrow I'll probably still be a dog. Sigh! There's so little hope for advancement."

Snoopy

H. Edward Wesemann

The Truth About Associate Marketing

Every year some firm asks me to speak to their incoming class of associates on how they should begin their business development efforts. For years I have pitched the standard techniques of personal marketing and, even as I was speaking, I could see that the seeds of the arguments they would spill back at me throughout their careers were already starting to germinate -- the top five reasons why associates can't develop business:

- "I didn't go to law school to become a salesman."
- "The firm values billable hours and I can't bill hours and develop business."
- "I have a (insert one) new spouse/young child/sick mother and my time outside the office is taken."
- "I'm an introvert by nature."
- "I don't plan to become a partner."

So this year I decided to take a different approach. I would present them with the keys to the kingdom, the veritable Rosetta Stone of the practice…in short, I would tell them the truth. I now repeat for you what I will tell this year's class of bright eyed and extraordinarily well paid associates.

There are three different strategies attorneys in a large law firm can employ to generate business. The first is *The Active Sales Mode*. This includes all the normal law firm marketing advice: constantly be on the look out for business development opportunities, become active in civic organizations and trade groups, write articles, give speeches, join country clubs, and hob-nob with people who can give you business. I confess that I don't personally know any associate for whom this has actually worked but, with perseverance, who knows what might happen.

Strategy two is to *Hitch Your Wagon to a Star.* Find a partner who has a big book of business and ingratiate yourself. A partner who is a couple of years from retirement or smokes heavily would be ideal. Then go about impressing that partner's clients with your legal mind and service ethic (most clients don't know torts from toothpaste, so you're better off with service). Wow them at every turn: deliver documents to their house at 9:00 on a Sunday night, send them clippings from their industry's trade magazines, remember their children's names and ask about them in every conversation. The more aggressive associate might consider suggesting to the partner's secretary that the client's phone calls be forwarded to him or her if the partner is not available. Pretty soon the client starts calling the associate directly. The partner's happy because the billing numbers are still showing up in her column and she doesn't have to bother with actually talking to the client.

The third possible strategy is to *Build Your Brand.* This involves deciding early on "what you want to be famous for."[1] Pick an area of law or an industry and become an expert in it. Unfortunately, it takes years of study and experience to become an expert in an area of law. But with a little time on the internet and a quick Nexis search you can pretty well bring yourself up to speed (i.e., know more about it than just about any of the partners) on most industries. It obviously helps if you select an industry that (a) is not ridiculously technical, (b) is somehow associated with your undergraduate major, (c) is related to work that you are doing and/or (d) you have a smattering of interest in. Then use every opportunity to broadcast your expertise within your firm by dropping industry jargon in conversations, submitting requests to attend industry conferences and sending unsolicited firm-wide e-mails alerting everyone to some seemingly important piece of breaking industry news. Pretty soon you're the firm expert on that industry. They may even build a practice group around you.

Now, while you ponder these alternative strategies, let me suggest the top ten things associates can do to develop business without really trying:

1. **Catalog your experience.** Once a quarter or so, take a half hour and go through your time records. Develop categories for clients you have worked for, what kind of matter it was and the types of services you performed. This will provide you with an honest and accurate assessment of your own experience and it will knock the socks off of the partner in charge of associates when you go in for your evaluation.

2. **Understand your client's business.** Every time you get an assignment, even if it is just drafting a form document, spend 10 minutes understanding the client's business by going to their web page, looking them up in Standard & Poor's or finding their ad in the yellow pages. Clients want and respect attorneys who understand their business.

3. **Take the Dale Carnegie Course.** Just trust me on this. There are valuable skills that they don't teach in law school. Forget Anthony Robbins. Nobody does it better than the folks at Dale Carnegie. They are listed in the white pages of the telephone book. The firm will probably pay for it and if they won't, it's most likely tax deductible.

4. **Read the front page of the *Wall Street Journal* every day.** The practice of law in most large firms involves the facilitation of business. To do this effectively you have to know what is going on in the business world. There is probably a copy in the library or you can swipe it from the reception area. Read at least the 2nd, 3rd and 5th columns.

5. **Get a life.** I once went to lunch with an associate and all he could talk about was the deal he was currently working on. He couldn't talk about sports, current events, movies, literature – nothing. The practice of law is a personal service business which requires that you must be a person, not just a lawyer.

6. **Keep in touch with your network.** Find a reason to stay in touch

with the people you met in school. Even the dolt you helped through contracts and the drunken sorority sister who threw up on your couch will eventually rise up the evolutionary ladder and land a position where they can be of assistance to you.

7. **Figure out what's hot and what's not.** Look down the road and figure out whether the area of practice you're in is growing or declining. A sure test is your hourly rate. If it is less than your peers, find a way to finagle yourself into a high rate area.

8. **Update your marketing bio quarterly.** Before you can sell yourself to clients, you have to sell yourself to your partners. When a partner puts together a presentation for a prospective client, you want him or her to have the most impressive resume of your experience possible.

9. **Communicate, communicate, communicate.** Don't just sit in your office grinding out work. Talk to your fellow associates, invite a partner you don't know to lunch (and don't talk about business) and generally create a presence within the firm. To use you and promote you, people have to know you.

10. **Actively manage your career.** Your firm may help but it can't and won't do it for you. Understand your strengths and weaknesses. If you don't like the work you are doing, tell someone. Set goals for yourself in every possible area. If you aren't getting sufficient feedback, go to the partner and ask specific questions.

If you do just these 10 things, you will be employing the best of all three marketing strategies and business development will never be a problem for you.

So that's what I told them. Will it do any good? Ask me in about eight years.

"USA Today has come out with a new survey –
apparently, three out of every four people make
up 75% of the population."

David Letterman

The Seven Basic Laws of Successful Networking

Most lawyers understand the importance of networks. For attorneys with a significant following of clients, much of their success is often the result of an active referral network of clients, friends and business associates. For many attorneys, particularly those with a transactional or regulatory practice, one of the most valued services they offer their clients is a large rolodex of contacts. There is probably no profession where the ability to effectively network is more important than the practice of law.

All over the country bar associations and chambers of commerce are holding networking events where eager participants can hand each other business cards. The theory is that when someone needs a lawyer, they will dig through their Palm Pilot to find the name of the person they met at last month's networking event. Could it happen? Sure, why not. Does it happen very often? Probably not.

There are some basic facts about networks that few attorneys take the time to appreciate. These are not how to techniques for working a room and remembering

75

people's birthdays. Instead, consider the seven basic laws of networking:

Rule #1: For many purposes, weak tie networks are more valuable than strong tie networks

There are essentially two forms of networks[2]. Strong-tie networks are made up of the people with whom you have a close relationship – people they see every day. Close friends, family members, other attorneys at your firm and clients may be members of an attorney's strong-tie network. Weak-tie networks are made up of acquaintances, school classmates, opposing counsel, and people you send Christmas cards to but never talk with otherwise, From a technical perspective, members of your strong-tie network are people with whom you engage in an ongoing exchange of resources. The exchange may be psychological, as between two close friends, or financial, as between a lawyer and a client. In a weak-tie network, the individuals know you and you know them, but, beyond that, there is no exchange of resources.

Let's consider an example of the use of strong ties versus weak ties. One of the classic uses of networks is finding a job. In a university study, two groups of people sought jobs using only network contacts[3]. One group used their strong-tie network exclusively and the other only used their weak-tie network. The default reaction of most people is to use their strong-tie network first and, if that didn't work, move on to the weak-tie network. Yet, the study found, quite convincingly, that the people who used their weak-tie network got higher paying jobs than those using their strong-tie network.

Although this result is not exactly intuitive, it makes sense when you recognize that ones strong-tie network is made up of the people with whom they have the closest relationships. But, because of the closeness of that relationship, you already know most of your close friends' closest friends and families -- the contacts of your strong tie next work end up being redundant to your own. As it turns out, the greatest value of a weak-tie is that it can bridge you to a whole new network of people.

But don't count out the value of a strong-tie network. Weak tie networks are fine for the small stuff – getting information, making introductions, cutting red tape – but for the really big stuff, you need a strong-tie network. Strong tie networks are made up of people from whom you can ask the big favor because it has been earned over years of exchanging resources, i.e., doing favors for one another.

Rule #2: People grossly underestimate the size and power of their existing network

How many people are in your network? I have asked that question to a significant number of attorneys in private practice and their answer seems to range from 200 to 1,000—rarely more. However, studies seem to indicate that an average professional has a weak-tie network of at least 3,000 and often as many as 10,000 people.

If a network of 10,000 seems impressive, watch this. If we use the bottom of the range and assume a person's weak-tie network is 3,000 people, and each of those people has a network of 3,000 people, a professional has access to a network of 9 million people who are just one link away. Of course the fallacy in this is that, even with a weak-tie network, there is some duplication of contacts. If one of your contacts is a partner in another law firm, it is likely that many of his or her contacts are people you already know. So, being super conservative, suppose that only one percent of the people in your contact's network are not duplicative to people in your network, the second link still produces 93,000 people and the third link is 86.5 million.

The fact is, most professionals don't need a larger network, they just need to better utilize the network they already have.

Rule #3: The diversity of a network is more important than its size.

Here's an example of the power of a weak-tie network. In the late 1960's, a group of sociologists conducted a study to see how many network ties it would take to accomplish a seemingly difficult task[4]. A group of people in Nebraska were each given an envelope addressed to a stockbroker in Sharon, Massachusetts. The only information they were given was the person's name, the fact that he was a stock broker and that he lived in Sharon, Massachusetts. Members of the group were not permitted to call information or look up the recipient's name in the telephone book. All each person could do was give the file folder to a person they knew (a member of their strong or weak-tie network) and ask them to give it to the best person they knew to eventually deliver it to the stockbroker. So, one person might give it to their stock broker who would send it to an acquaintance in Boston, who would send it to his stock broker, etc. It took an average of only six links to have the file delivered. The speed with which a joke gets passed around on the internet and the popularity of the play, *Six Degrees of Separation,* may cause this small number of links to be less surprising today than it was in the 1960's. But the fact remains; there are just six links between any two people drawn at random from 250 million.

The reason why diversity is important is the degradation that occurs in a network when one increases the number of links. Suppose that I want Michael Jordon's autograph. If I have a contact who knows Michael Jordon, the chances of my getting the autograph are greater than if my contact has a contact who knows Michael Jordon. And my chances are really low if my contact has a contact that has a contact, etc. The more diverse the network, the more likely I can accomplish my objective with a single link or, at most, two links.

A second reason for the diversity of a network is the dilemma of multiple contacts in an organization. The common view is that the more contacts one has in an organization, the better "wired" they are to accomplish their objectives. But, if, for example, you are seeking an introduction to the general counsel of a major corporation and you have several contacts at that company, your chances of obtaining the introduction are probably not made significantly greater by having multiple contacts. In fact, there are often situations where attempting to use multiple contacts within one organization to achieve an objective can actually be counter productive and destructive to the relationship with all of the contacts. Better one strong-tie contact to an organization than a bunch of redundant weak-ties.

Rule #4: Before a network contact can be of value to you, you must have proven your value to them

Now comes the tricky part. Just because you have a weak-tie relationship with someone doesn't mean that person is going to be willing to allow you to use that relationship. Casual awareness of each other by two people does not create a functional network contact. The process of creating a network is one of developing a relationship with an individual at a minimum and, to create some exchange of resources. The process must, therefore, be bilateral, i.e., for me to become one of your contacts, you must become one of mine.

This bilateral nature of a network relationship is often difficult for people to accept. For example, suppose you meet an accountant at a business event and you exchange business cards. A month later, you remember that one of the accountant's clients is a company with which one of your clients would like to do business. If the depth of your relationship is one meeting and an exchange of business cards, the likelihood of your being able to effectively use this contact on behalf of your client is pretty slim. On the other hand, if a couple of weeks after you met, you sent an email to the accountant, advising him that one of your contacts is working on a small acquisition and may need some accounting assistance, you have now exchanged a resource with the contact (even if the lead does not turn into business for the accountant).

The key to network building is creating a series of unfulfilled *quid pro quo* situations. In the army, one of the most valuable soldiers in a company is the "scrounger." As typified by the character of Radar O'Riley in *MASH,* scroungers are able to accomplish almost anything through their network. But it is never a direct quid pro quo relationship (if you do this, I will do that). Instead, sociologists tell us that in almost all societies, people feel the need to discharge obligations. So using a network is a process more involving providing contacts with the opportunity to discharge an unfulfilled *quid pro quo* than of "calling in markers."

Sociologists refer to the favors performed in these exchanges as "currencies."[5] These currencies can take all sorts of forms, including assistance in performing some task, helping your contact expand their network or just acts of personal kindness. The key is that the best network builders are those who go about looking for opportunities to earn the contact relationship by fulfilling one of the contact's needs without seeking a direct reciprocation. It is a subtle form of what Marlon Brando does in the *Godfather* movies when he says, "some day, and that day may never come, I will call upon you for a favor…"

Rule #5: The best network contacts are at your own level

The default reaction of most people is that contacts should be at the highest levels possible. In fact, the most beneficial contacts are at peer level or below. The reason is the difficulty of creating a resource exchange with someone far above your organizational level. Supposed a lawyer is invited to lunch and has occasion to sit next to the CEO of a Fortune 500 corporation. They have a pleasant conversation, exchange business cards, and agree to call each other for golf "sometime." The difficulty is what kind of "currency" can the lawyer use to create an unfulfilled *quid pro quo* for the CEO? Worse, it is likely that the CEO is actually at too high a level to be functionally useful in assisting with routine matters and the tie is not strong enough to ask for something really big.

But you have to careful about what you consider peer level. For example, it would be easy for someone to ignore networking opportunities with contacts who are of a different economic status, age, race, or gender. This diversity, however, is precisely what helps create the most effective networks.

Rule #6: Contacts require constant attention

Not surprisingly, contacts deteriorate in direct proportion to the weakness of the tie. As much as people talk about old school ties, it is difficult to call up someone who you have not talked to in years and expect their assistance. The same is true for unfulfilled *quid pro quos.* The value of the exchange currency spent on a relationship diminishes rapidly and rarely lasts at all after one year.

The result is that effective network users devote substantial efforts to maintaining and expanding their networks, seeking ways to fulfill their contacts needs and creating exchange currencies. In fact, studies show that as much as fifty to sixty percent of successful professionals' time is spent on activities that could be considered network building.[6] It seems impossible that a fully productive lawyer could devote this much time to networking and still meet their client responsibilities and billable hour targets. In fact, what happens is that networking becomes a natural part of what successful lawyers do and becomes integrated with billable activities and avocational time. As one successful lobbyist/lawyer put it, "constantly working my network is as natural to me as breathing."

Rule #7: Design networks to eliminate structural holes

Because creating and maintaining a network is such hard work, the long term functionality of the network is important. In the course of building a network, it is easy to end up with a single contact as the tie to an entire network. For example, suppose a lawyer builds a contact relationship with the Executive Director of a trade association and, through that contact, is able to access contacts throughout the industry. The network works well so long as the link to it is in place. But, if the contact were to leave his position, the entire network is in jeopardy. The answer is to create a network with redundant links. The charts below show two networks, one with structural holes and the other without structural holes. In the left diagram, if Ed were to leave his position a hole would be created and Bill would lose all access to the Ed's network. In the right diagram, Bill has three points of contact to the network.

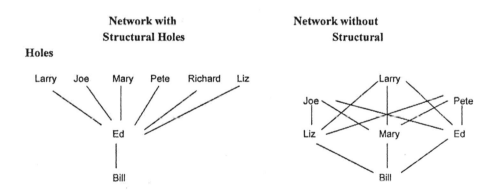

Diversity in networks is good, but never to the point where there is a single link to the network.

The Rules of Networking

These seven rules represent the difference between a successful and functional network and a bunch of names in a Palm Pilot. Networking requires such a high degree of effort and can be so important to the success of a professional that it only makes sense to do it in the most effective way possible.

"I don't know the key to success, but the key to failure is trying to please everybody."

Bill Cosby

H. Edward Wesemann

When Good Law Firms Go Bad

In the last few months the unthinkable happened. Brobeck, Phleger & Harrison, Arter & Hadden and Altheimer & Gray -- three of the largest, and seemingly, the most stable law firms in America -- voluntarily closed their doors. They didn't restructure; there were no death knells. They dissolved – puff, they were gone.

The Obituaries

Brobeck was the epitome of a large successful law firm. One of the most powerful firms in San Francisco and an innovative national leader, Brobeck had been selected by *Fortune* magazine, at the end of 2000, as one of the "100 Best Companies to Work For." Innovative special-effects ads graced national television. The 77-year-old firm was viewed as the future of legal practice and was one of only a handful of firms to successfully create a brand identity for itself. From 1998 to 2000, the firm skyrocketed to over 900 lawyers and $476 million in revenue, then, in 2003, plummeted to dissolution.

Cleveland-based Arter & Hadden carried 160 years of tradition and experience, as well as a highly regarded reputation in the Midwest. It was routinely ranked by *American Lawyer* magazine as one of the fastest growing law firms and was historically known as a fiscally prudent firm with a close-knit culture that laterals raved about. In the 1990s, the firm began significant expansion in California and by 1999 peaked at almost 500 lawyers with $146 million in revenue. The firm ceased operations July 15th.

Altheimer & Gray pioneered growth in emerging markets in central Europe and embraced the challenges of the global economy. The aggressive and entrepreneurial international firm yielded large profits from its transactional practices in third world countries and held strong political contacts in Chicago. It peaked at 200 lawyers in Chicago and 100 lawyers in eight other countries in Europe and Asia. Just last September the firm expanded to San Francisco. On June 27th the executive committee voted to dissolve.

So what happened? These firms had generations of experience in dealing with law firm challenges. The media explained away the failures in typical business terms. Accustomed to reporting on corporate failures, they accepted the easiest answers and pronounced the dissolutions as being caused by excessive debt, too rapid expansion and the impact of the national technology slump.

Was the media right? Certainly the technology slump can claim its share of negative economic influence. And no one can explain away the millions of dollars in debt and explosive expansion. Yet, are these problems markedly different from the challenges confronting the majority of other large law firms? Are all law firms headed for bust as a result?

Let's consider debt load. According to an article in *The American Lawyer*, which cited a confidential Citibank survey, Brobeck's debt load of $277,000 per-equity-partner was nearly identical to the average $272,000 per-equity-partner debt load of comparable Silicon Valley firms. And for New York firms, that average debt load jumped to $409,000 per-equity-partner. It would appear that extensive debt was hardly the decisive firm-busting enemy the media and some consultants have made it out to be.

Let's consider expansion. These firms proceeded at much the same pace as their peers on the AmLaw list of largest law firms. All large national and international firms expand, and they all, especially the ones that have been around for generations, know how to handle the peaks and valleys and accompanying debt that follow such expansion. Just look at the success of London's "Magic Circle" firms like Clifford Chance that have grown almost geometrically.

Certainly the impact of the slow economic recovery and the technology slump must be a cause. With such a dismal economic year and technology's profound influence on legal success, you'd expect this year's AmLaw numbers to have plummeted, especially considering the six percent decline in average gross revenue of Fortune 500 companies, right? Guess again. Last year, profits-per-equity-partner increased 6.9 percent, gross revenue increased 8.5 percent and revenue-per-attorney increased four percent. Not to mention that weathering the rise and fall of practice areas and financial cycles is a routine challenge faced many times before by these firms.

So really... What happened?

Maybe Greed isn't Good

In the 1980s money movie, *Wall Street*, Michael Douglas, as slick financier Gordon Grecco, richly expounds, *"Greed is good."* After all, the reason corporations are in business is to increase shareholder value. It's all about money – always has been, always will be.

But professional service firms, particularly law firms, are different from corporations in several important ways. No significant permanent asset base – retained earnings -- exists to cushion law firms' "bad years." And law firm shareholders all show up for work every morning, deriving the bulk of their income from a single investment. When ownership is involved, business becomes more than merely a financial investment. Law firm ownership involves a culture and camaraderie that transcends financial issues.

The proverbial wolf was not at the door of any of the three firms that went under. None of them were insolvent. What happened is that profits declined. Owners weren't putting as much cash in their pockets. According to the American Lawyer, in 2002 Altheimer & Gray saw a 12.9% decrease in profits coming off of a record year in 2001. Arter & Hadden's profits were only down 6.5% from an above average year. In fairness, Brobeck was down 38.6% but it ended up paying $26 million in income to the bank instead of to partners. Still Brobeck's profit per partner for 2002 was a not too shabby $420,000. What happened was the firms simply didn't generate enough cash to compensate the owners at the level to which they had become accustomed.

So what's the big deal? Business is all about putting capital at risk, isn't it?

Changing the Glue

Well, not when the end result is an entire change in the basis for being. Law firms that traditionally stressed trust and shared a vision for the future became short-term, profit-focused financial engines. Perhaps the culprit wasn't the notorious debt associated with rapid expansion, but the notorious greed associated with such success. The insatiable appetite for more strayed the firms off course – leading them away from their decent, if not noble, purpose. Partnerships that took pride in "taking care of each other" became meritocracies where the measure of worth was "how much have you done for me lately."

And the partners in these firms began dropping like flies. Among the casualties -- Brobeck lost its chairman and 54 lawyers who went with him to a rival firm. Arter and Hadden lost dozens of partners with big books of business. And Altheimer and Gray lost the key player behind their profitable international practice, as well as suffering defections within their government relations department.

The simple fact is that when a firm makes it all about money, little else matters. And it is then that the capital at risk becomes a big deal. When you create an organization where the major focus is the maximization of profit, you must expect that when the profits are greater somewhere else, that's where the partners will go. When you see a firm like Arter & Hadden lose half of its partners and a huge chunk of its largest business generators in a two-year period, or like Brobeck, where the managing partner led a major defection, only one explanation is left -- "If the only reason I am here is money, then why wouldn't I go where the money is better, even if it's only a little better."

The high-profile demise of Brobeck, Arter and Altheimer drags a startling trend to the surface. The lesson to be learned has nothing to do with debt or growth or economic declines and everything to do with tying people together with a shared vision, purpose and culture. Without this, firms lose their ability to weather the inevitable storms, something these particular firms had generations of experience in doing. Money can be an important part of the vision, but it has to be the result of achievement, not the purpose for being.

In law firms, money can be good – greed can't.

H. Edward Wesemann

"Art is making something out of nothing and selling it."

Frank Zappa

H. Edward Wesemann

Mergers as a Marketing Tool

When most firms bring their Marketing Directors into merger discussions it is to capitalize on the publicity value of the event. But in doing so, the firms are missing the boat on the biggest marketing benefit of a merger -- the opportunity for their lawyers to actually go out and talk to their clients.

This is not to say that there is no place for public relations initiatives in announcing a merger. A well written press release and a good relationship with the media may get the merger a feature story on the business page of the Saturday edition of the local paper. You might even get a mention in national legal publications.

But in these days of multi-hundred billion dollar corporate mergers, a couple of law firms getting together usually draws a "ho hum" from most editors. The real "win" for merging law firms is the opportunity it provides for their lawyers to meet with their clients and tell them about the merger and the advantages it offers to them as a client of the new firm.

As any seasoned Marketing Director knows, most lawyers will go to great lengths to avoid face-to-face marketing to a client. They much prefer to create glossy brochures, hold seminars and generate name recognition in hopes that clients will voluntarily call them seeking their services. However, we know from experience that when a lawyer meets with a client, particularly at the client's place of business, the frequency with which the lawyer comes back with new business is higher than with any other form of marketing.

So the most important marketing value of a merger is to create a reason for the firm's attorneys to personally announce the merger to the firm's clients and to develop the discipline to ensure that these face-to-face meetings occur.

The results can be extraordinary and can easily outstrip any of the planned synergies discussed during the merger talks. To obtain the greatest marketing advantage from a merger, the marketing department must be sure that two things occur:

- every attorney (and staff member) in both firms must have a clear understanding of the benefits of the merger, and
- a detailed plan must be developed to assure that the appropriate client contacts are made.

On the Same Page

The basic motivation for virtually every law firm merger is the hope that two plus two will equal five, and that five will mean greater profitability for the firm. To add up to five, the merger must create some value to clients that is not present before the merger. Otherwise, the merger doesn't make a lot of sense.

The marketing department should identify those client advantages and package them in an understandable, rational explanation for the firm's lawyers to tell their clients. In most cases, these benefits are spelled out in the presentations made to the partners of the two firms when they vote on the merger, but often the issues discussed before the vote center on the financial and operational aspects of the merger. The job of the marketing director is to get the attorneys to focus on the benefits-- from the client's perspective which usually involve the addition of new practice capabilities, greater depth in important practice areas and/or greater geographic coverage.

Getting everyone to sing from the same hymnbook can be difficult. One easy way to do it, especially in a multi-office firm, is to create a short video of the managing partner in which he / she discusses the critical issues that will impact clients. The tape need not be professionally made and can even include a mock client meeting during which a partner explains the benefits of the merger to the client. If the video is played at an attorney meeting in each office, enough copies should be dubbed for distribution to attorneys who do not attend. Whether or not a video is used, each attorney should receive a page of talking points highlighting the most important advantages of the merger to a client.

It is important that the attorneys are prepared to answer the most common questions that clients will have:

- Now that you're a larger firm, will your rates go up? This is especially important if the merger involves a small or boutique firm.
- Will you (the partner announcing the merger to the client) still be the attorney representing me?
- Does the merger create any conflicts that I should be aware of?
- How are you going to make this work? Clients are business people and are often curious about the details of a merger – where will the offices be located, whether the firm will be reducing staff and similar questions.

The Rollout Plan

Simply equipping the attorneys with a story to tell is not sufficient. The marketing director has to make sure that the information actually gets to the clients. Timing is everything. No client wants to think that he or she is the last to know about a merger, but you can't contact everyone at once. Here are some tips on rolling out the information:

- Prepare a model letter for each attorney to send to his or her clients. Ideally the letters should go out on the day the merger is announced. The letter should not delve into the reasons for the merger, but should say that the attorney will contact them within the next couple of weeks to schedule an appointment for an in-person meeting. The letters should be individually signed by the attorney responsible for the client relationship.
- Develop a list of the merged firms' clients by responsible attorney and identify those who are likely to derive the greatest benefit from the firms' expanded capabilities.
- Create a plan and schedule meetings for the first six to nine weeks after the merger. List clients to be visited by each attorney and, when appropriate, make it a team visit with an attorney from the merged firm or from a practice area that provides a cross-selling opportunity.
- Work with the attorneys' secretaries to make sure the meetings get scheduled. Check back with the attorneys at the end of each week

95

to make sure the meetings occurred and to solicit feedback. A few success stories will do wonders to motivate recalcitrant partners.

- Prepare a weekly communications piece (memo, e-mail or newsletter) to talk about the number of clients visited, typical client reactions and new work generated.

- Develop a list of targeted *potential* clients who might benefit most from the new capabilities of the combined firm. Circulate the list among the attorneys to obtain possible points of contact and develop a plan to contact potential clients after current clients have been visited.

Of course, the marketing department must also handle other merger related projects. But hour for hour, the time spent preparing and encouraging your attorneys to use the merger as an opportunity to create face-to-face contacts is the most productive use of time.

"Here's something to think about: How come you never see a headline like 'Psychic Wins Lottery'?"

Jay Leno

H. Edward Wesemann

Trends that Will Affect Law Firms Over the Next Five Years

1. **Lawyers' undergraduate majors will become as important as where they went to law school.** The practice of law will become increasingly technical as the most profitable areas of practice shift to intellectual property and technology related industries. Just as intellectual property attorneys with electrical or ceramic engineering undergraduate majors have been in high demand for the past couple of years, lawyers with scientific (especially biology and chemistry) engineering, accounting, e-commerce and other functional backgrounds will be prized in the future.

2. **The organization of law firms will shift from practice groups to industry group.** For years clients have told their lawyers that they want to be represented by people who know their business. Lawyers will finally listen and begin organizing themselves around their clients. But this shift won't be primarily marketing oriented. The need for technical expertise by account managing partners will naturally drive these lawyers together by their common interest and their

need for each others knowledge. Look for the relationship lawyer to become more of a multipurpose legal specialist in the client's eyes. The same micro-biologist lawyer, who runs your corporate legal work, does your IP and your litigation, supported by service attorneys with practice expertise.

3. **KM will go the way of TQM and Y2K.** As good as knowledge management sounds on paper, it doesn't work for sophisticated law firms. Partners won't support it because they fear it cheapens their value within the partnership by giving away their knowledge to "competing" partners. Lawyers won't depend on it because the information the computerized codifications spit out won't be quite on target and they will prefer personal conversation with an experienced lawyer ("talking to the chef rather than reading the recipe."). Most importantly, firms will find that after spending millions on programming and codifiers, they have no way to recover the cost from clients. Worse, clients, although they talk a good game, may select a firm with a great knowledge management system in place for commodity work, but it won't be a differentiator for the most sophisticated (and profitable) work.

4. **Strategic planning is dead.** The days of the grand, soviet style, comprehensive strategic plans are over. Most law firm strategic plans are internally focused on organizational and operational issues. As competition for the best work increases (because consolidation has decreased the number of clients and law firms) how firms position themselves in the marketplace and beat out their competitors will become vital for the survivors. All the black magic of SWOT analysis and mission statements will be pushed aside for leadership driven external strategies. Look for firms to focus on one or two strategic issues and devote their efforts and resources to them over tight time frames.

5. **It's all about culture.** As growth and consolidation brings strangers into partnership with each other, preserving or creating firm culture will become a dominant internal issue in law firms. Lessons learned from Enron and Arthur Anderson will put the firm's culture onto the front burners with a particular point of how firms enforce their core values and deal with rogue partners. Culture will be the number one

retreat topic for the next few years.

6. **Employment practices will replace malpractice as an issue that keeps risk management partners up all night.** With more firms seeking employment practices liability insurance, the disclosure of prior occurrences on insurance applications is going to disclose many firms' dirty little secrets. In addition to the ever present sexual harassment problems, employment discrimination, wrongful discharge, and failure to partner are now joined by stressful workplace issues. The total of dollars spent on claims within the retention level and the premiums for insurance will put things like diversity training at the same level with professional liability programs.

7. **CEO style managing partners will be replaced by more decentralized authority.** The combination of the lack of accountability in most law firms, the increasingly disperse geographic office structures and the media coverage of corporate CEO's escorted to jail in handcuffs will cause many firms to change their collective vision of the ideal leadership structure. Firms that have strong managing partner systems won't change back but many firms that are attempting to move further in that direction will find large executive committees and strong practice leaders back in vogue.

H. Edward Wesemann

Notes

(Endnotes)

[1] "What you want to be famous for" is an idea that David Maister came up with in his book, *True Professionalism.* There's probably a copy in your firm's library or spring for $24 and buy a copy yourself.

[2] The concept of strong and weak networks and much of the thought process behind this article is the product of lectures by Professor Joel M. Podolny at the Stanford Graduate School of Business.

[3] Mark Granovetter, Getting a Job: A Study in Contacts and Careers, University of Chicago Press, 1995.

[4] Stanley Milgrim and Jeffrey Travers, "An Experimental Study in the Small World Problem," *Soclometry*, 1969.

[5] David L. Bradford and Allen R. Cohen, *Organizational Dynamics,* Winter, 1989.

[6] John Kotter, "What Effective Managers Really Do," *Harvard Business Review,* 1982.

.

About the Author

H. Edward Wesemann is a consultant to some of the largest professional service firms in the world. A partner in Edge International, Ed's consulting practice specializes in assisting professional service firms with strategic issues involving market dominance, office location, merger and acquisition and the activities necessary for strategy implementation. With over 20 years of experience in working with law firm strategy, Ed has worked with firms ranging from 25 attorneys to several thousand.

He holds a Master Degree from Roosevelt University School of Business and a Bachelor of Science in Business Administration from Valparaiso University. Recognized internationally as the foremost expert in law firm culture, Ed developed the use of the Edge International Cultural Inventory as a means for law firms to understand and manage the way members of their firm relate to each other, clients, and the business environment. In 2001 he wrote the definitive article on law firm culture in Legal Management magazine. The article has since been republished in Europe, South Africa and Australia. Ed and his wife Janice reside in Savannah, Georgia.

Printed in the United States
25511LVS00002B/63